COUNSELING THROUGH BIBLE NARRATIVES

OLD TESTAMENT

THE ASSOCIATION OF BIBLICAL COUNSELORS
General Editor SHAUNA VAN DYKE

COUNSELING THROUGH
BIBLE NARRATIVES
OLD TESTAMENT

THE ASSOCIATION OF BIBLICAL COUNSELORS

ISBN 978-1-7344406-2-1

TABLE OF CONTENTS

TABLE OF
CONTENTS (cont)

"God gave us the Bible not just to inform our minds, but also to transform our hearts."
– John Piper

The Bible is the authoritative Word of God, so the life-giving truths we find in Scripture is sufficient for all matters of life and contains all that we need in order to know God's will and live a life pleasing to Him.

> *All Scripture is breathed out by God and profitable for teaching, for reproof, for correction, and for training in righteousness, that the man of God may be competent, equipped for every good work* (2 Timothy 3:16-17).

In your call to counsel, the Bible equips us for good works and gives us practical principles to help others live out in obedience to God. As we encourage others to surrender and submit to Scripture it will transform their hearts, which allows them to grow in spiritual maturity. My prayer is that this book will offer a simple and efficient way to gain understanding of God's Word, strengthen the way you counsel and equip you to speak the truth in love. May you be blessed as you walk others through Bible narratives found in the Old Testament, ministering in the relatable and raw moments of their story.

I am incredibly grateful the Lord gave me this assignment and for the support of my brothers and sisters in Christ. It is a privilege to work alongside so many gifted teachers and counselors. My prayer is we will later expand this book while also creating additional resources using other books of the Bible. A huge thank you to all my friends in ministry who participated in this project and to the ABC team for your continued support.

Your sister in Christ,

Shauna Van Dyke

INTRODUCTION

THE INEVITABLE IMPACT OF NARRATIVE *By Jeremy Lelek*

Narratives are part of the human condition. Our lives are an unfolding narrative, a story written on the pages of the heart. Some of these stories are tragic and devastating. Others are soaring, beautiful narratives that bring hope. Each person you encounter in counseling has a narrative. What makes us effective counselors is how well we read these narratives. The reason so many come to us is because they have become lost in the pages of their own stories. Many attempt to write their own script, their own narrative instead of trusting the narrative written by the Holy Spirit. Those we serve in counseling have formulated narratives that shape their lives, perspectives, and habits—often unaware of the impact that these internal stories have on their experiences of being in the world. Christians who live in the West exist under what James K.A. Smith calls "a brass heaven" wherein the narratives historically shaped by transcendence are often mere whispers when compared to the modern narratives shaped by the immanent or material-commercial here and now. [1]

Self-help books, commercials, therapy and exercise programs, news outlets, Netflix, Facebook, Twitter, Tic Toc, and Snap Chat are all propagating narratives, and as far as the social media platforms are concerned, we are free to create any public narrative of our choosing. Furthermore, watch the most popular news outlets (especially in the United States) and you will quickly experience the power of narratives on what we believe, and how such narratives shape our perspectives, opinions, and habits—even our emotions—on a mass scale.

The inevitability of narratives is why it is so vital to utilize the narratives of Scripture in our counseling practices. These stories, unlike those propagated under Smith's brass heaven, reconnect us to transcendence reminding us that He (God) is there and He is not silent. [2] God has spoken, and one of the means by which He has chosen to communicate is through narrative. He has done so from the beginning.

Consider the first two people to whom God communicated: Adam and Eve. God revealed his love and goodness by blessing them with everything they needed (Gen. 1:27–1) with one caveat: "And the Lord God commanded the man, saying, 'You may surely eat of every tree of the garden, but of the tree of knowledge of good and evil you shall not eat, for in the day that you eat of it you shall surely die" (Gen. 2:16–7). God's narrative is, "I am your good, trustworthy, and faithful Creator and Provider." It was a narrative that if believed and operated from would have blessed Adam and Even with ongoing life and peace. God's narrative was the true narrative, but there was one in the garden who introduced a different story—a different gospel.

The serpent was cunning. He knew to ask Eve the precise question that could potentially change the narrative God had spoken to her. "Did God actually say, 'You shall not eat of any tree in the garden'?" (Gen. 3:1), and then answered his own question to further embody in Eve an alternative narrative potential: "You will not surely die.

---

[1] James K.A. Smith, *How (Not) to be Secular: Reading Charles Taylor* (Grand Rapids, MI: William B. Eerdmans Publishing Co., 2014), p. 2.
[2] Francis A. Schaeffer, *He Is There and He Is Not Silent* (Wheaton, IL: Tyndale House Publishers, 1972).

For God knows that when you eat of it your eyes will be opened, and you will be like God, knowing good and evil" (Gen. 3:5). On this account, Matthew Lapine cites one theologian who notes that "...the temptation narrative is a conflict of interpretation. The serpent takes God's place as the epistemic authority by reinterpreting his speech; the issue is not autonomy." [3.] In other words, Satan's narrative becomes the narrative Eve believes as final truth, therefore shaping her perception of God from that of being good, faithful, and loving to being dishonest, untrustworthy, and ultimately uncaring for her wellbeing. The embrace of this reinterpreted narrative shaped Eve's sense of being in the world (from theocentric to egocentric), impacted her belief system about God and what is good, and ultimately influenced her motivation to blatantly disobey the most loving Being that exists. Narratives matter.

From the garden on, God spoke to his people in ways that formed God-centered narratives, accounts that now serve as historical narratives that may serve to shape our perspectives, beliefs, desires, and habits. The volume you are reading is the attempt of the *Association of Biblical Counselors*—with help from our members, partners, and friends—to provide readers with helpful counseling resources drawn from Old Testament narratives. The handouts in the book will assist counselors on points to cover in session with counselees as well as provide "after session" homework for them to work through.

Our prayer is that the narratives highlighted will help counselees embrace and assimilate life-giving, Godspoken stories that may serve to bring new perspective, and therefore renewed hope in the One who spoke them.

[3.] Matthew A. Lapine, The Logic of the Body: Retrieving Theological Psychology (Bellingham, WA: Lexham Press, 2020), p. 256.

GENESIS 3 1-10

SHAME DESTROYS AND CHRIST RESTORES

By: Shannon Kay McCoy

www.shannonkaymccoy.com

Adam and Eve were living in perfect harmony with God, themselves, and each other. They were fully known by God and one another. Deceived by Satan, they committed a soul-damaging sin and hid from God. Immediately their nakedness was exposed, and shame clothed them. In this bible narrative, we see how God pursues those cloaked in shame to cover them with His righteousness.

IN SESSION COUNSELING
Read Genesis 3:1–10

What exactly was the lie Adam and Eve believed?
- Adam and Eve knew what God said (Gen. 2:17) and Eve repeated it to the serpent (Gen. 3:3). They were not to eat from the tree of the knowledge of good and evil because they would surely die.
- The crafty serpent told the truth that the forbidden tree would give them knowledge of good and evil. The exact lie the serpent told to the woman was, "You will not surely die" (v. 4). This lie led them to spiritual death—separation from God.
- Have you ever been deceived into believing a lie about God? Have you ever doubted what God has told you as truth?

Why did Adam and Eve hide from God?
- In Gen. 2:25, Adam and Eve were both naked (unclothed) and were not ashamed. Nakedness was not a sin because it represented innocence.
- Adam and Eve's disobedience caused them to lose their innocence and they became guilty and ashamed. Now their nakedness represented sinfulness.
- Their eyes were opened, and they perceived their nakedness as sinful. They felt exposed and hid their shame. Shame is the realization of something disgraceful, vile, and detestable whether it be done by oneself or by someone else.
- Adam and Eve's perception of their nakedness exposed their guilt before God and ushered in the devastating consequences of judgment, condemnation, and death.
- How have you responded to your sense of shame? In what ways have you hidden from God?

How did God rescue them?
- God pursued them in their shame (v. 9). The awareness of their shame caused them to cover themselves and hide from God, who came looking for the relationship he once had with them.
- God graciously covered their nakedness and shame (v. 21). Shame is the loss of the glory God intended His creation to display. This glory is restored by the shed blood of Jesus Christ, offering redemption and reconciliation to God (Col. 1:20).
- Jesus came to seek and to save those who have lost their innocence and who are shrouded in shame (Lk. 19:10). Jesus calls the shamed to fix their eyes on Jesus because He has conquered all sin and shame (Heb. 12.2).
- In what ways have you tried to cover your shame? Have you put your trust in Jesus who has conquered your shame?

AFTER SESSION ASSIGNMENT

1. Read and reflect on Hebrews 12:1–2. When the weight of shame crushes you and you want to hide from God and others, what should you do instead?

2. Pray. Confess your shame to the Lord and receive His covering of grace.

GENESIS 6 5-9

DEPRAVITY OF MANKIND

By: Dr. Ray Hicks
www.SV.church

Genesis 6:5–9 drives home the extent of our sin nature and sinfulness. In it, we are confronted with the depravity of mankind in Genesis, as well as with a glimpse of our own depravity. The author of Genesis rips from the headlines of our hearts when he writes, "every inclination of the human mind was nothing but evil all the time." Just read a daily paper or watch a newscast and you will see this clearly.

Quickly following, we read some of the most crushing words in Scripture when Genesis 6:6 states in, "the Lord-Yahweh regretted that he made man," and, the Lord-Yahweh "was deeply grieved." That "deeply grieved" phrase drives conviction into our hearts and causes us to ask ourselves, what have we done in our lives and relationships to grieve, to wound and to break the heart of God?

Then, we read a hopeful passage for all of us in Genesis 6:9 when the writer states, "Noah was a righteous man, blameless among his contemporaries; Noah walked with God." These words make us ask ourselves if we are a people whose hearts seek God's righteousness, and if, like Noah, we strive to walk blamelessly among our contemporaries. This leaves all of us with two heart questions about our lives. First, do we grieve and wound the heart of God by our actions, thoughts, words, and behaviors? And, secondly, do we allow God to reign in our hearts and yield our wills to Him so that we can walk blamelessly with Him before our contemporaries?

The biggest struggles of our lives are always heart struggles because that is where we make those self-centered decisions we find in Genesis 6:5–7. At the same time, we are able to make those Christ-centered decisions and find favor with God as Noah did in Genesis 6:8–9. So, just like Noah and the people of his day, we have the ability to pursue evil and every inclination that fills our hearts, or we can pursue God like Noah did and find favor with Him and walk blamelessly before those all around us.

God desires each of us to do the hard heart work of repentance, faith, and sanctification as we surrender daily to His will in our lives, our words, our thoughts, our relationships, and our behaviors. Let's be faith-filled and careful that we not grieve and wound the heart of God, but instead recognize God's kindness, mercy, and grace toward us.

IN SESSION COUNSELING

Read Genesis 6:5–9 aloud and have the counselee(s) answer at least two of the following questions:

1. What area of your life or relationship issue do you think grieves the heart of God?

2. What area of your life causes you to grieve?

3. Is there sin in your life for which you need to repent?

4. What heart changes will help you restore your love relationship with the Lord?

FOR THE COUNSELOR

If the counselee confess that he/she knows of things in their life that have grieved and wounded the heart of God, you will need to do three things:

1. You will need to help them pray a prayer of confession of their sin toward God.

2. Next, the prayer should include pleading for God's forgiveness for each specific sin. This is because we sin specifically, and therefore, we must confess and seek forgiveness specifically.

3. Then, you will need to help them pray a prayer of repentance as they turn from sin and walk toward God seeking His will in their lives and walking rightly in His favor.

You will need to affirm their desire to begin a new daily walk with the Lord with specific faith steps to walk away from how they were grieving God, and to begin a new daily walk with Him with all their heart, mind, soul, and strength. This should include Bible study, prayer, praise, and community worship.

AFTER SESSION ASSIGNMENT

Ask the counselee to read one chapter of Ephesians each day. When they finish the epistle, I have them start over again. I have them do this for one month journaling their answers to these questions each day: 1) What is God showing me about Himself? 2) What is God showing me about myself? and 3) What heart changes does God want me to make in my life from my reading?

GENESIS
37-47

JOSEPH: BEING MERCIFUL

By: Michael Van Dyke
www.truthrenewed.org

The narrative of Joseph is remarkable with many applications, but one of the most formidable is Joseph's display of mercy primarily due to his trust in God's providence. Joseph's account is sketched through the last thirteen chapters of Genesis. Under God's sovereign hand, Joseph experienced difficult offenses at the hands of his embittered brothers, being estranged from his family in a foreign land, wrongfully imprisoned, and ignored by those whom he helped while imprisoned. At the end of his providential suffering, Joseph becomes the second most powerful person in the known world. He uses it as an opportunity to be merciful and be reconciled with his family who would become the nation of Israel.

To be or become the recipient of leniency and compassion is a way mercy could be defined. Another way to think of mercy is that it's a quality of compassion, especially as expressed in God's forgiveness of human sin. Scripture stresses God's forbearance toward sinners. In his mercy, God shields sinners from what they deserve (which is death) and gives gifts that they don't deserve (which is grace). Mercy is not getting what we do deserve (His wrath) and Grace is getting what we don't deserve (His love). All of this comes from the attribute of his goodness.

Prior to session: Have your counselee read Genesis Chapters 37–47 prior to your session and write out the things they learned about Joseph and about mercy. Note: There is a lot to cover within this narrative, so you may not be able to cover all of it in one session.

IN SESSION COUNSELING
Discuss the takeaways that your counselee had about Joseph and how mercy was shown. Take time listening to discern their understanding and then walk through the moment of mercy points below.

Moment of Mercy:
Relational conflict is the most significant opportunity for mercy. The brothers' hatred motivated their action to kill Joseph, and now mercy's motivation is to reconcile the relationship (Gen. 37:3–28).
* How many estranged relationships do you have that can be reconciled through being merciful?

Moment of Mercy:
Being merciful isn't at the expense of truth, but trusting in God as our final judge and trusting him with the consequences. In other words, when someone wrongs us, we don't have to go to the nth degree to make sure every bit of truth is exposed and demand justice, but rather, trust in God's timing and rest in him as the just and justifier (Gen. 39:1–20).
* When was the last time you overlooked an offense? Read Proverbs 19:11.

Moment of Mercy:
Even when relationships feel inconsequential, mercy is an opportunist waiting with gifts of compassion. When life happens, and relationships become work, we tend to convince

ourselves that there is just too much going on to work on our relationships, so we become stagnant. Being merciful is taking the initiative and bringing words of healing to a life of hurt, even when we're the ones who've been hurt (Gen. 39:21–40:4; 40:14–15; 41:9; 41:14–16; 41:32–33; 41:37–45; 41:56–42:25).

* What relationship(s) do you need to take the initiative toward, bringing healing words to a life of hurt?

Moment of Mercy:
Mercy is dependent on relationships; we can't be merciful without them. Mercy can't be demonstrated without us being in a relationship with others. Frequently, when others' actions hurt us, we just remove ourselves from them, thus removing ourselves from opportunities to be merciful as God is merciful. Luke, in his gospel, calls us to be merciful as our Father is merciful (Gen. 42:26–47:31).

* Have you convinced yourself that you've forgiven them for the offense, transactional mercy, but haven't pursued the relationship with grace and compassion, maybe toward your spouse or friends, where you have a low-functioning contempt toward them that you need to confess and be reconciled?

Moment of Mercy:
Godly mercy doesn't end with forgiveness but begins with it and progresses into a life-giving relationship. In other words, the purpose of extending mercy is to have a relationship. When Joseph made himself known to his brothers, he didn't just forgive them, give them grain, and tell them to be on their way. That would have been simply transactional mercy, but he started there and then gave them lands in Egypt to ensure relationship: the full measure of mercy. Another example would be feeding the homeless; we're moved to compassion to see their state of life, and we want to feed them so they don't go hungry, so we provide for them. If that's all we do, we're showing transactional mercy, which is good, but it's not complete mercy. Imagine if God just forgave us of our sins but didn't pursue a relationship with us through the Holy Spirit (Gen. 42:26–47:31).

* Are there people in your life that you distanced yourself from because they hurt you and you haven't pursued the relationship since the offense?

Counseling Takeaway:
Joseph sees his brothers as they bow before him, requesting grain, and he deals with them harshly. They still do not recognize him, and Joseph puts them through a test to bring his youngest brother back to Egypt. His brothers go back as they were instructed, and after some struggle from Jacob, they come back to Egypt with Benjamin, their youngest brother, and the prayer of Jacob asking for God's mercy before the man. They go before Joseph a couple of times, once to eat, from which Joseph removes himself briefly due to compassion toward his brothers. Then he tests them again, they go back to his father, they come back, and then he breaks down, makes himself known, and embraces them. Then he shares with them how he understood God's plan of using their hatred as a means to produce good and preserve God's people. So, they reconcile, and Joseph calls for all of them to move to Egypt and settle in the land of Goshen to have a relationship with them.

AFTER SESSION ASSIGNMENT

Read Genesis 37–47 again and journal through the questions we discussed during our session. Take time praying and listening as God reveals how you've received mercy and ways you can show mercy to others.

NOTES

GENESIS
37-50

STEWARDING POWER WELL

By: Brad Hambrick
www.bradhambrick.com

The story of Joseph is not a simple, flat story. It is a complex story that spans a lifetime. It involves family drama, multiple betrayals, and political theatre. The story of Joseph is no simple children's story and would not be something you could fully review in one counseling session. I would begin by asking the counselee to read the narrative, Genesis 37–50, prior to your counseling session. This will allow you to accomplish more depth in the conversation as you discuss the powerful example of forgiveness and restoration.

IN SESSION COUNSELING

Now that the counselee has already read the narrative, use the session time to discuss the points below and help them apply the truth within their specific struggle.

Begin by tracing the theme of power throughout the story.

Initially, Joseph has the power. He is his father's favorite son (Genesis 37:1–11). This means he doesn't have to do the worst family chores and he gets nicer clothes than his brothers. *Joseph does not steward his power well.* Actually, he's a jerk. He flaunts his power and chides his brothers. By modern, American legal standards, Joseph's actions were *interpersonally offensive* (i.e., rude). We would say he needed to repent, but we would not call the police.
• Do you have power in your relationship(s)? Do you flaunt your power or steward it well?

Later, Joseph's brothers have the power. They out-number Joseph, they are older, and they are physically stronger than Joseph. *Joseph's brothers do not steward their power well.* They beat their brother, throw him in a well, and sell him as a slave (Genesis 37:12–36). By modern, American legal standards, Joseph's brothers' actions were *criminal* – kidnapping and human trafficking. We would say they needed to repent, <u>and</u> we should call the police if we learned of comparable actions.
• Is there someone in your life that uses their power against you? In what ways?

In the final scene, Joseph has the power again. He is second in command to pharaoh and controls the distribution of grain during a famine (Genesis 42–50). *We applaud Joseph because he is the first person in this sequence who uses his power to bless and redeem instead of abuse and demean.* Reading this part of the story, we want to be like Joseph and want everyone else to be like Joseph, too. When we hear from someone who has been through hard times, as Joseph went through hard times, Joseph comes to mind as a great example to follow.
• What are ways you or others could use God-given power to bless and redeem?

Within that power, Joseph responds with forgiveness and restoration.

When Joseph famously says to his brothers, "What you intended for evil, God intended for good (paraphrase of Genesis 50:20)," two interpersonal activities are occurring: forgiveness and restoration. Because these two responses so frequently travel together, we can easily view them as two sides of the same coin, rather than independent actions. *Forgiveness* is the removal of relational debt. *Restoration* is engaging a relationship as if the relational debt did not occur. To illustrate the difference, if you allowed a friend to borrow your car and they wrecked it by driving carelessly, forgiveness would mean not requiring them to pay for damages, but restoration would mean letting them borrow your next car. You might do one without the other.

- Explain your understanding of the difference between forgiveness and restoration.

In Genesis 50, Joseph is both forgiving his brothers (not throwing them into prison) and being restored to his brothers (inviting them back into family relationship). It was good for Joseph's soul to forgive his brothers. It honored God and gave Joseph freedom from bitterness. We can say with confidence that this is what God wanted for Joseph. We can also say with confidence that God was patient with the journey. It took Joseph 13 chapters (Genesis 37–50) and approximately 24 years (best guess from Bible scholars) to come to this place of forgiveness. We should be equally patient in advising others to forgive. Why was restoration wise for Joseph, and when would it be wise for us? We notice that before Joseph restored relationship with his brothers, he took steps to vet whether greed, power, or fear would cause them to relapse into their old pattern (Genesis 44). He wanted to be restored, but he also wanted to be wise.

- Who in your life do you need to forgive? Is there someone you have forgiven but the relationship is not yet restored?

AFTER SESSION ASSIGNMENT
Journal through the things we discussed in session today and the questions below. Return with your responses in our next session so we can work through them together.

1. Make a list of relationships in your life where forgiveness is needed. What relationships have not yet been restored?

2. Is there someone currently in your life that is abusing their power over you?

3. What hurts and offenses are you holding on to?

4. What is a key takeaway after reading about Joseph?

GENESIS 50

15-21

FREEDOM IN FORGIVENESS

By: Andrew Dealy

www.austinstonecounseling.org

Forgiveness is a thread knit throughout the pages of God's word from Genesis to Revelation. Without it, the Bible would have wrapped up in Genesis 3 right after the consequences of sin. It is because of God's kindness, patience, and forgiveness which are all born out of His love that we have the rest of the story and the hope of redemption. Joseph's story, recorded in the later chapters of Genesis, particularly displays what it looks like for us to forgive others as God has forgiven us. In this lesson we will seek to understand and apply a biblical approach to forgiveness.

IN SESSION COUNSELING
Read Genesis 50:15–21 and work through the following:

At times we are all like Joseph's brothers believing that what we have done is impossible to forgive. So, we find ourselves manipulating situations in order to avoid retribution. We respond just like Adam and Eve when we see our sin. We hide, minimize, deceive, and blame-shift.

- **Are there things currently in your life that you are afraid to confess and ask forgiveness for because of fear of how the person may respond?**

- **Are there sins you have committed that you find yourself justifying or minimizing?**

- **What steps is God inviting you to take in these situations?**

Joseph's response is remarkable. He has clearly been shaped through the crucible of his suffering and it has left him kind, patient, and empathetic. Joseph doesn't mince words when he identifies what his brothers did as evil. Yet their intentions are not the primary lens through which Joseph sees life. If it was, the natural response would've been bitterness and vengeance. Instead, Joseph looks at his brothers and his circumstances through God's eyes. Forgiveness requires these two things: 1. We truthfully acknowledge the evil done. 2. We recognize God is at work as we faithfully seek to respond to others as God has responded to us.

- **When others have wronged you do you tend to minimize what they have done? Why is minimizing unhelpful?**

- **Are their areas in your life where you are struggling with bitterness? What is shaping the way you view those situations?**

In forgiveness we refuse to define people solely by the wrongs they have done. No doubt this is us treating others as we ourselves long to be treated. Such forgiveness frees us up to love those who have hurt us and enables us to see them as more than the pain they have caused. This is beautifully displayed in Genesis 50:21 as Joseph not only forgives his brothers but also promises to care for them and their children.

- Do you find yourself defining people in your life based on the hurt they have caused you?

- What step could you take to show love to those who have hurt you?

AFTER SESSION ASSIGNMENT

1. Forgiveness is hard and costly. The most perfect picture we have of forgiveness is Jesus choosing to die on the cross for our sins. Nothing about that could be described as easy or cheap. So, I want to invite you to take some time and pray that God would cultivate a heart of forgiveness in you. Be honest with the Lord about why this feels difficult and ask Him to help you see yourself and your situation with His eyes.

2. Read Matthew 6:5–15. Pray that God would bring to mind situations in which you need to ask for forgiveness and extend forgiveness. Write these down and ask yourself what the next step of faith is that God is inviting you to take in each situation.

3. Read 1 John 1:9. Take time to meditate on God's forgiveness for you. He knows all you have done and still deeply loves you. Dwell on this until your heart warms to this truth. He loves you and does not define you by your sin.

EXODUS 15

19-27

GOD OUR HEALER

By: Emily Dempster

www.shccounseling.org

The people of Israel spent many years under great oppression. From sunrise to sunset, they labored hard in the hot sun in the field making bricks for the Egyptians. They worked rigorously and yet they were beaten and whipped on a regular basis. God provided the timing and protection for Moses to lead them out of slavery to freedom and the Promised Land. Beyond the Exodus and through the miraculous crossing of the Red Sea, the children of Israel found themselves in the middle of the desert without any water, only to be led to the bitter waters of Marah. Why would God lead them there?

IN SESSION COUNSELING

Read Exodus 15:19–27 aloud and discuss the following three responses.

Response 1:
Miracle of the Red Sea (v. 20–21).
- In what ways did the Israelites respond when they got through the Red Sea?

Response 2:
Desert and Bitter Water at Marah (v. 22–24).
- Describe the scene in the desert. What was their response to this situation?

Response 3:
God's Response to the People (v. 25–26).
- How did God provide?

Counseling Takeaway:
Soon after God provided healing for the Israelites with the sweet water, he led them to Elim, which is believed to be 8 miles from Marah. God provided 12 springs of water and 70 palm trees — an oasis in the desert. God could have easily led the people to the oasis first. However, God saw the people's heart and wanted them to see their own heart too. God will not always lead us straight to Elim, but He always has in mind to use the bitter waters we encounter to show us our heart and to point us to Him.

EXODUS 15:19-27

AFTER SESSION ASSIGNMENT

1. What are the bitter waters you are facing right now (physically, spiritually, emotionally)?

2. How is your response similar to or different from this story?

3. Pray the words of Psalm 139:23–24 as you reflect.

JUDGES
4 & 5

DEBORAH: FAITH IN THE LORD'S STRENGTH

By: Jay Younts
www.Everydaytalk247.com

Deborah was a wife, a prophet, a judge, and referred to herself as a "mother in Israel." It was by God's particular choice that a person was a prophet or a judge. We learn from this narrative that God used a woman to display His great power and lead Israel. Deborah demonstrated that she was committed to God and did not go beyond God's command or created order. This is what gave her strength. Deborah becomes a role model for all women, not so much for the offices that she held, but for her great faith and trust in God. She demonstrated the courage to obey God first.

A pattern in Judges is that Israel continues to turn from God. The judges are an indication of God's mercy. The Israelites have been under the control of Canaanite king Jabin and his general, Sisera, for twenty years. The Lord speaks through Deborah and she instructs Barak to plan an attack on Sisera. But, Barak is fearful and does not trust the word of the Lord that came through Deborah. So, he demands that Deborah go with him to the battle. She agrees but says that the honor will not go to him, but to a woman. That woman's name was Jael. Deborah urges Barak to strike (v. 14). He does and the battle is won. However, Sisera escapes and goes into Jael's tent where Jael, also showing great courage, kills him. Deborah's prophecy was fulfilled: Barak led the army to victory. Sisera was killed by a woman, and the Israelites were freed from their enemies.

In chapters 4 & 5 we gain a complete picture of what happened. Deborah's song in chapter 5 is a mixture of praise, narrative, and triumph. The song praises God and shows the harshness of living in a sin-cursed world. Deborah teaches us that God's word can be trusted in the face of great adversity. She and Jael are women who show the power that comes from believing and trusting God's word. After the battle, Israel had peace for 40 years.

IN SESSION COUNSELING

Read Judges chapters 4 and 5 with your counselee, and then together discuss what you learn from this narrative. Focus your discussion on what is producing fear in the counselee's life.

Two women believed God stepped out in faith and did what others were afraid to do.
- Have you ever been called to step out in faith? To attempt the unexpected?

God often accomplishes His plan by using the least expected.
- How have you felt undeserving in your calling? Have you been surprised in times when God has used you? Are you struggling now, feeling unworthy or insecure?

It sometimes requires great risk, sacrifice, and effort on our behalf to serve and trust the Lord.
- Do you have any fears that are holding you back? What do you have a hard time letting go of?

We should rejoice in the Lord when He delivers us from oppression. Remember that praise means repeating back to God the great things he has done. Psalm 78:4
- How do you rejoice in the Lord? Through worship, prayer, serving others?

AFTER SESSION ASSIGNMENT

This week reread Judges chapters 4 and 5, and review the questions we discussed in session and those below to seek the Lord's strength and plan for your life.

1. How does this narrative encourage to you step out in faith?

2. How do you see women differently after reading this narrative and how God used Deborah?

3. What kind of accountability, support or new habits can you put in place to help you eliminate your fears and walk in faith?

JUDGES
6-8

GIDEON:
FEAR TO FAITH

By: Todd Hardin, PhD
www.thinkingchristianly.com

The book of Judges begins with Israel's falling away from God. The story presents a cycle in which the Israelites forsake God (by doing what was right in their own eyes; see: 17:6; 18:1; 19:1; 21:24; and 21:25), become oppressed, call out to God, receive God's deliverance, enjoy prosperity, and then inevitably forsake God yet again. It is in this context that we read about a fearful man named Gideon.

Gideon's story opens with Israel under Midianite oppression. An angel of the Lord approaches Gideon and promises that God is with him. But that is not all. The angel also refers to Gideon as a "valiant warrior" (see 6:12). After bestowing this moniker, the Lord commissions Gideon to drive out the hated Midianites. Gideon hesitates because he doesn't feel up to the task nor worthy of the name.

However, the Lord is patient, and through a series of tests, He proves the authenticity of both his word and Gideon's commission. The time comes and He calls Gideon to lead Israel into battle. Knowing Gideon's fearful nature, at this pivotal moment the Lord suggests one more test. He encourages Gideon to go on a reconnaissance mission and discover what the enemy thinks of Israel. Gideon does. And there, in the stillness of the night, Gideon overhears a man describing a dream about a great Israelite victory. Another man interprets the dream and Gideon learns that this victory came about by something called "the sword of Gideon" (see 7:14)! This is the turning point of Gideon's faith (see 7:15). From that moment on, God progressively transforms Gideon from a man of timidity to a man of decisiveness. God continually fills Gideon with the Spirit and Gideon consistently yields to that filling. As a result, God brings about a miraculous victory through Gideon.

God rewards Gideon's obedience with forty years of undisturbed prosperity in the land (see 8:28). Alas, as is common with all of us, the children of Israel fall back into the same old bad habits. Instead of following God, every man does what was right in his own eyes (Judges 21:25). As such, the cycle starts over.

The Gideon story reminds us of how anxiety comes in cycles. It affects how we see ourselves, others, and even God. So often, those who come for counseling struggle with their identities. For a multitude of reasons, people often have a distorted view of self. For the most part, they can function in life pretty well; however, when confronted with difficulties, they tend to withdraw into themselves and seek refuge behind a wall of anxiety and self-loathing. As counselors, we need to encourage them to break free from their self-imprisonment and help them see themselves the way God sees them.

IN SESSION COUNSELING

The story of Gideon in Judges 6 through 8 provides an anchor that allows counselees to tie their personal narrative to the biblical story. As the counselor, educate and elaborate. Gauge the counselee's biblical literacy and meet them where they are. Don't just lecture. Instead, tell the story, listen well, ask good questions, and guide your counselee toward these main points:

- God is the hero of the story, not us.
- What God thinks of us is more important than what we think of ourselves.

- As we learn to trust God, he will sharpen our faith.
- As God sharpens our faith, we will experience critical moments that will change the direction of our personal stories.
- As we appropriate these turning points into our personal narratives, our faith will deepen, and we will become progressively more action-oriented and less anxiety-driven.

AFTER SESSION ASSIGNMENT

After the session, have the counselee give you an initial summary of the most important thing he or she learned from this exercise. Then, assign the following homework:

1. Before the next session, I want you to read and meditate daily on the Gideon story in Judges 6 through 8.

2. As you work through these chapters, identify key connections between Gideon and yourself. In other words, be able to reflect and identify the answers to these questions:
   - How am I like Gideon at the beginning of the story?
   - What does God think of me based on his Word? (Give scriptural evidence here).
   - What challenges am I facing? In other words, "Who are my Midianites?"
   - What "turning points" has God revealed to me? Said another way, "What *Judges 7:15 Moments* have I experienced?"
     » How have I responded to those moments?
     » Now that I am aware of these inevitable moments, how do I plan on responding to them in the future?
   - How can I specifically respond like Gideon as I continue dealing with my Midianites?
   - If I am obedient, how will I be more like Gideon at the end of the story?

3. What specific, concrete changes do I need to make so that I can live up to the God-bestowed title of "valiant warrior?"

Work with the counselee to brainstorm specific ways he or she can deepen their faith so that they can live out their newly discovered identity in Christ.

NOTES

JUDGES 13-16

FINDING VICTORY OVER HIDDEN SIN

By: Chara Donahue

www.shccounseling.org

Even strong individuals can find themselves in destructive relationships, as the narrative of Samson illustrates so well. Samson habitually chose women who were not suitable for him according to God's Word. They came from pagan families and lived in ways that showed they worshipped other gods: power, money, and control. Strong, but habitually attracted to making an idol of his significant other, Samson shows us the dangers of letting a fallible person control our lives more than God. He is an excellent case study of someone who is weak in standing up to his significant other but shows strength in other areas of life.

IN SESSION COUNSELING

Recap Judges 13–14: An angel appears to announce that a barren woman and her husband will soon become parents to Samson, who God has declared should live under a Nazarite vow. As an adult, Samson rebels against his parents' wishes in his choice of a wife by saying, "Get her for me, for she is right in my eyes" (Judges 14:3). Disaster, death, and destruction unfold as Samson's new wife betrays his trust. She is killed by the Philistines and Samson slays 1,000 Philistines with a donkey's jawbone. No contemporary could match the God-given strength of Samson and he leads Israel as a judge for 20 years—until he meets a woman named Delilah.

Read Judges 16:4–22

What behavior patterns do you see in Delilah?
Delilah uses Samson's love for her to wield power and control over him. Patterns of manipulation exercised to gain power and control can easily turn abusive and should be confronted with healthy boundaries. Boundaries are set to protect, not to control. Boundaries help bring some order to the chaos that a counselee may be experiencing. Genesis 1 shows God setting boundaries in creation, and Mark 10:35–45 shows Jesus drawing boundaries with the disciples.

Does Samson seem ignorant or aware of these patterns?
What patterns do you see in him?
Samson seems to be aware of the patterns but still trusts Delilah with his secret even though she has repeatedly betrayed him. He either decided to hope in her against all evidence or got so tired of the game she was playing that he just gave in to her wishes. Both of these actions are evidence of an unhealthy relationship, and evidence that he was not looking to God to guide him into wisdom.

How does Samson's willingness to allow these patterns to exist in his relationship work for him?
Samson's willingness to enable destructive patterns and live in the deceptive light of "love is blind" left him literally blind and enslaved.

What advice would you have given Samson after Delilah's second betrayal?
We forgive sin, fight off sin, call out sin, but to blindly overlook chronic sin in the name of love is something we must not do. We serve the God who can redeem all things, and we have to understand that we can only confront the dangers of darkness by bringing them into the light.

AFTER SESSION ASSIGNMENT

Unhealthy patterns can be repented of and toxic relationships can heal, but if we let love blind us to the weaknesses and failings of our object of admiration we do not fully love. Instead, we end up in a relationship not based on reality but fantasy. True love sees and loves still. Take the time to prayerfully reflect on the patterns in your own relationship.

1. What behavior patterns do you see in your significant other?

2. What patterns do you see in yourself?

3. How can you seek God to help you break free from these patterns? Write one step you can take this week and be ready to discuss how it went in your next session.

4. Read Mark 10:35–45 and Mark 12:13–15, 24–27. How did Jesus draw boundaries with those he interacted with?

JOSHUA 7

ACHAN: STRONG BUT WEAK

By: Chara Donahue
www.lifeaudio.com/the-bible-never-said-that

It is much easier to hide our sin than to confront it, but often in counseling, we help people recognize and repent from sins that hurt themselves and their loved ones. Other times we walk alongside someone who has been caught in sin they were trying to hide. They need to hear the truth to combat lies they have been believing. The narrative of Achan and the Valley of Achor can be a poignant signpost to the need for gospel redemption and timely repentance of sin. It explores the ill effects of hiding transgression, the sobering consequences of sin, and the hope available to those who seek Christ for forgiveness.

IN SESSION COUNSELING

Recap Joshua 6: In Joshua chapter 6 the walls of Jericho came tumbling down. God was clearing the path to the promised land. Jericho was a major city protected, armed, and strong. With God's power behind them, the Israelites conquered this civilization with ease as they obeyed the strange but powerful commands of the Lord. Their faithful commitment soon faltered due to one man's greed. God commanded the Israelites to destroy everything from the city as an offering to Him, taking nothing of what remained for themselves. When God leads us victoriously through battles we still must stand firm against temptations that come with that victory.

Read Joshua 7:1

Achan's sin remains hidden until the Israelites go to conquer Ai. They find that the Lord's anger burns against them. Ai should have been conquered easily, but instead, Israel is defeated due to the sin festering in the camp. Joshua calls out to God and asks him why, and God tells Joshua to stand up, get off his face, and find the offender.

Read Joshua 7:16–26

Who did Achan's sin impact?
We are deceived if we believe that hidden sin will not impact the lives of people around us. It hurts our family, our neighborhood, and the community at large. Sin against God, even sin that seems like it won't affect others, is still an offense against God. Sin's impact cannot be isolated; we still suffer the consequences of Adam and Eve's sin.

Look carefully at verse 21. How does Achan's sin progress?
Scripture clearly says that Achan saw, coveted, took, and hid. It is easy to fall into this pattern with sin. We must learn to identify and cut off temptation before it progresses.

How might Achan have rationalized his sin?
Rationalizing sin is one of the most deceptive tendencies our imaginations engage in. Embracing God's view about sin and circumstances helps us fight off the false scenarios we create in our thoughts.

How do you feel about the severe consequences for Achan and his family?
Romans 6:23 teaches that the wages for sin are death, and that the outcome is clear in this narrative.

We must not take sin lightly. Our sinful acts required a supreme payment and cost the life of God's son to satisfy the debt owed. He paid the most precious price so we could be rescued from the consequences we deserve. "For our sake he made him [Jesus] to be sin who knew no sin, so that in him we might become the righteousness of God" (2 Corinthians 5:21).

As soon as the sin was dealt with, the Israelites overcame Ai. What victories could you have if you let go of the sin in your life?
We are not designed to carry hidden sin within us. The Spirit of God will always war against the darkness in our lives, and we will feel confused, agitated, and fearful within if we are concealing something the Spirit is battling to bring to the light. If we harden ourselves against the promptings of the Spirit we will feel anxious, despondent, and far from God—for we have told him we don't want to hear from him.

Achan's sentence was carried out in the Valley of Achor which translates to the valley of trouble! This valley had seen sin and death, but what does God do with this desolate place in Hosea 2:14–15?
God is faithful to forgive us (1 John1:9) when we confess our sins. Just as with Israel, he can open a door of hope for us in the middle of our trouble if we seek him and follow his leading.

AFTER SESSION ASSIGNMENT
Read 1 John 1:5–9 and work through the below questions. Journal and bring back any reflections you might want to discuss in your next session.

1. If we say, "We have no sin," we are deceiving ourselves. How does this passage instruct us to deal with the sin in our lives?

2. In what ways have you tried to rationalize your sin?

3. Take some time confessing to God the ways you have walked in darkness and read verse 9 again.

4. God promises to forgive our sins and cleanse us from ALL unrighteousness because of the work of Christ on our behalf. Do you believe this?

5. How can you walk further into the light today?

1 SAMUEL 25

PREPARING FOR THE PROPER USE OF LETHAL FORCE:
BUILDING SPIRITUAL RESILIENCE IN MILITARY AND LAW ENFORCEMENT PERSONNEL

By: Curtis Solomon, PhD

www.solomonsoulcare.com, www.biblicalcc.org

When Abigail intervenes to rescue her family from David's murderous rampage her insightful speech offers us wisdom and an example to follow. Her words warn David of severe consequences to his soul if he does not turn away from his plan to kill Nabal. She does not condemn David for killing in general; in fact, she praises his military campaigns carried out on behalf of the Lord. What she warns against is killing out of selfish motive and vengeance. This narrative offers a great example of what we might call "pre-counseling" or "preparatory-counseling." Abagail is used by God to prevent David from experiencing deep guilt and distress for shedding blood unjustly. You can use this text with people serving or considering service in the military or law enforcement. People authorized to use lethal force may face the temptation to abuse this authority. The text demonstrates that killing in the line of duty for just reasons is a righteous activity that God ordains and approves. However, killing for selfish or unjust reasons will result in guilt and a disturbed soul even if one escapes legal consequences. The text also highlights the fact that the temptation to misuse lethal force is often heightened when we are grieving the loss of a loved one.

IN SESSION COUNSELING

Read 1 Samuel 25 and then discuss the following questions:

1. Does Abigail condemn every act of violence or killing that David has done or will do?

2. What does she warn against?

3. What does Abigail say will happen if David does not change course and proceeds to kill Nabal for selfish reasons?

4. What factors might be influencing David to react so harshly when we have seen him behave with much more restraint in the past when faced with worse threats?

5. Imagine a scenario in your career field where one of your comrades has been killed and you are tempted to pursue and kill the person or people who killed him. What could you think to yourself and do to prevent yourself from giving in to that temptation? Take some time to discuss this with our counselor and write down some of your thoughts.

AFTER SESSION ASSIGNMENT

1. Read the following biblical texts to consider how they influence your understanding of the use of lethal force: Genesis 9:6, Romans 13:1–5.

2. Take some time to write out a clear plan of action to resist the temptation toward vengeance killing. Pray and ask God to help you respond in this way if you ever encounter that situation. Share your plan with one to three close friends who can pray that for you as well and help keep you accountable to it.

3. List some other temptations you may encounter in your career field and begin to develop similar plans to counter them.

NOTES

1 SAMUEL 25

A GODLY WOMAN AND BIBLICAL RESPONSE

By: Laura Chica
www.r3stored.com

The 25th chapter of 1 Samuel tells the compelling narrative of a wise woman who demonstrates a biblical response to two angry men. This narrative is instructive to those who may be struggling with both ungodly and/or godly relationships and how to biblically respond to each.

IN SESSION COUNSELING

Read 1 Samuel 25, and discuss with your counselee the main characters and the points to consider. Then take time reviewing the following questions, asking your counselee to take notes as you review together.

Main Characters
- Nabal is an ungodly man who does what is right in his own eyes.
- David is a godly man who submits to what is right in God's eyes.
- Abigail is Nabal's wife who chooses to intervene with wisdom and discernment on behalf of her ungodly husband's decision . She also appeals to David, a godly man, to respond to Nabal's ungodly response with grace and mercy. Abigail demonstrates a beautiful example of a biblical response to both men.

Points to consider
- Nabal wrongs David by not paying David and his men a measure of food and resources for their protection in the wilderness.
- David becomes angry (James 1:20) when Nabal refuses to acknowledge their service and intends to take revenge on Nabal by killing all the men of his household (Proverbs 14:12).
- Abigail intervenes on Nabal's behalf. Against his directives, she takes responsibility for his wrongs, and makes amends for his offenses.
- Abigail, with great humility, appeals to David by reminding him of who he is in God's eyes and how he should respond biblically to Nabal's offense by not exacting revenge or spilling blood (Romans 2:4).
- David's heart is touched by Abigail's words and turns toward God (Acts 3:19).
- David blesses Abigail for her faithfulness and godly response.
- Nabal gets drunk and parties with his cronies.
- Abigail assesses the circumstances and chooses to address the issue with Nabal after he is sober.
- Abigail explains her actions to Nabal, telling him what she has done on his behalf to waylay his destruction and the destruction of his household.
- Nabal's heart gives out in his shock and dies a few days later by God's sovereign intervention.
- David marries Abigail.

Questions to discuss
- How is each character's relationship with God reflected in their behavior?
- In what ways do Nabal, David, and Abigail demonstrate their love, or lack of love, for God and for others?
- What risk did Abigail take by opposing Nabal's decision to not give a tribute to David and his men?

- What risk did Abigail take by approaching David on his way to destroy Nabal and his household?
- What did Abigail believe about God that enabled her to act with such boldness in her communication with both men?
- In what ways did Abigail appeal to David's heart for God?
- Abigail disobeyed her husband's command; what about her actions makes them a godly response?

AFTER SESSION ASSIGNMENT

Read 1 Samuel 25 again and look back at your notes from the counseling session. Journal the questions below and return with them to our next session.

1. What stands out to you from what you and your counselor reviewed in session?

2. Which character best reflects your own heart: Nabal, David or Abigail?

3. Are there any relationships in your life that are causing difficulty?

4. What wisdom can we glean about how to respond biblically to both a godly and an ungodly person?

5. Has the Lord revealed anything new to you through this narrative that you'd like to share with your counselor?

1 KINGS19 *1-18*

FRAILTY THY NAME IS HUMAN

By: Eliza Huie
www.elizahuie.com

1 KINGS 19:1-18

Following a fantastic victory in which the LORD, through Elijah, defeated the false prophets of Baal, when the people saw the defeat they fell on their faces claiming, "the LORD, he is God" (1 Kings 18:20–29, 39). This infuriated Jezebel, the ruling king's wife, who had a reputation for disposing the prophets of the Lord (1 Kings 18: 4, 13). In chapter 19 we see that even the most effective believers (Elijah) are prone to incredible times of weakness. In this narrative, notice how the Lord responded to the frailty and weakness of Elijah and consider how this can be encouraging for people who are depressed, discouraged, and wanting to give up.

IN SESSION COUNSELING

Read 1 Kings 19: 1–18. Use the points below to start a conversation. Reflection questions are provided to help guide you.

What does the passage teach about our humanness?
* *Confidence is fleeting if it is not in God alone.* Our expectations of being used by God may need to be challenged. Elijah expected the hearts of the leaders would be changed after the victory recounted in chapter 18. Elijah's confidence was in a plan. not in the God of the plan, which led him to feel hopeless.
  Reflect: How might your own discouragement be connected to the feeling that God does not seem to be following through with the plans you thought were his?
* *Wanting to isolate or give up when faced with discouraging circumstances is tempting.* When the heart of the king and his wife were not changed, Elijah felt as though all that had happened was for nothing. He separated himself from the person who could support him (his servant), isolated himself far from others, and determined it was better to give up.
  Reflect: Do you pull away from people when you are discouraged? Have you ever been so discouraged you felt like following God was pointless or that life was not worth living?
* *When you are discouraged, recognize the multifarious factors that may be at play.* Elijah needed to be reminded of who God is and the importance of trusting him alone. He needed a spiritual reset in this moment of despair. But for that reset to happen, he needed to be alive. When Elijah's plan was to go into the wilderness to die, God had another plan. God was invested in his life and he showed this by sustaining it. God tenderly drew near to Elijah and met his physical needs. God provided comfort and food. He cared for his human needs, but he didn't stop there; he attended to his spiritual needs as well. In caring for him, God was teaching Elijah who he is.
  Reflect: What does this section of the narrative teach you about what you might need during times of spiritual discouragement? How does seeing God's attention to Elijah's humanness encourage you?

What does the passage teach about our God?
* *God does not address us one-dimensionally.* God sends an angel and provides for Elijah's human needs. He does not condemn his human frailty. The angel affirms that this is too much for Elijah and provides what is needed.
  Reflect: How does seeing God's attention to human needs help you in your struggle?

- *In the highs and lows God is always teaching us who he is.* In chapter 18 Elijah had experienced the victorious power of God at Mt. Carmel and he appeared to have unshakeable confidence in God. But that was quickly followed by a significant downturn as we see him running to the wilderness to die. But God can turn a wilderness and a cave into a sacred space to draw near and teach us more about who he is. God did not wait for Elijah to be more useful to meet with him. He met him in his frailty. God is with us in the times we seem most effective and the times when we feel we can do nothing at all.

  Reflect: Do you feel like you must be useful to God in order to get his attention?

- *God keeps his promises.* After God attend to Elijah, talked with him, and showed his power to him, he tells him that he still has a plan (vs.18). God's plans were still being accomplished even if Elijah thought they had failed.

  Reflect: What can you do to remind yourself of God's promises during challenging times?

What does the passage teach about the gospel?

- God is a holy and powerful God, and we must all stand before him in judgment. He reminds Elijah of this in the cave when he told Elijah to go out of the cave and "stand before the Lord" (vs. 11–12). As Elijah stood sheltered by the firm rock of the mountain, a strong wind, an earthquake, and a fire hit the rock of the mountain and yet Elijah was safe. Elijah was not safe through his own ability to withstand the full force of the wind, earthquake, or fire. He was safe because of the shelter of the rock. We, like Elijah, must entrust our lives to God who provided a Rock (Jesus) who took the full force of the wrath of a holy and powerful God and made a way for us to come to him. Let this passage be a reminder of God's provision to save us and because of that, we now have a relationship with God who knows our frame and speaks gently to us.

AFTER SESSION ASSIGNMENT

1. Take time to read 1 Kings 19:1–18 again this week. Ask the Lord to help you see how he cares for his discouraged servant. Allow the attention God gives to Elijah's human needs to guide you. Consider what physical and emotional needs you may need to attend to as you face struggles. Attention to your physical and emotional needs may help prepare you to better attend and address spiritual matters.

2. Review the "reflect" questions in the sections above. Choose two or three of them to use as journal prompts and allow yourself space to write out anything the questions reveal. Share what you wrote in your next counseling session.

1 KINGS 19 1-8

GOD AS COMFORTER AND SUSTAINER

By: Alicia McCamy
www.sohillscc.com

Elijah had this incredible show of faith in front of the prophets of Baal. He believed in the power of God over the false gods of other nations. In a truly miraculous showing, God lights the altar created by Elijah on fire that was soaked with water, as the false gods remain silent and the false prophets are embarrassed. The story takes an interesting turn as we see Elijah in fear for his life because of Queen Jezebel, the wife of King Ahab, and he runs off to the wilderness for safety. For counselees struggling with fear, worry, and anxiety, through this story they will be able to see God's character shine through as comforter and sustainer.

IN SESSION COUNSELING

Read 1 Kings 19:1–8 and discuss the following:

In verses 1–3, can you relate to Elijah's fear and if so, in what ways have you become fearful and weary in your own life?
We know that Elijah is a prophet of God and a man of big faith, but even in the moments when we feel like our faith has been the strongest, difficult circumstances and situations can lead us to grow anxious and afraid. We know that the threat from Jezebel is a legitimate one, as she killed other prophets of God. Elijah could have been confident in God, who had already shown himself trustworthy, but like many of us he felt depleted and anxious.

How does Elijah respond to his fear in verse 4? How are you responding to the fear and worry in your own life?
Elijah not only runs from the situation, but we actually know he ran just about as far away from Jezebel as was physically possible and remain in the territory of Israel. He then cries out to God in a display of complete and utter hopelessness.

God hears the cries of Elijah and sends an angel to care for him. How does God practically care for Elijah in verses 5–7? How has fear taken a physical toll on your body? How can you better care for your body as you work through anxiety?
The angel comes to provide food, drink, and rest for Elijah. God sees how Elijah has been mentally, emotionally, spiritually, and physically drained and goes about meeting those needs one by one. Our God is patient and kind toward us when we struggle (Romans 2:4) and bears our burdens with us (Matthew 11:28).

We see in verse 8 that the nourishment Elijah received from the angel will sustain him on a journey to speak with God. In the verses that follow, God will speak to him again and provide him instructions. At times we have to care for our bodies in order to get to a place where we can again hear God and his word.

Counseling Takeaways

We are body and soul and we must attend to both when we find ourselves in a place of worry, anxiety, and fear. God has designed our bodies to be physically sustained by rest, food, and water. As we begin to address physical elements, it will help us to better address the spiritual elements we are struggling with. We can better face suffering and fear when our bodies are being tended to properly. We then bring ourselves to God's word and truth to inform our thoughts and feelings of the greatness and power of God over all circumstances.

AFTER SESSION ASSIGNMENT

1. What in your life is causing you to feel weary and anxious? Bring these to God by journaling out specifically what is bogging you down.

2. How have fear and worry had a physical impact on your body? Consider your sleep and eating habits. What changes can you make in these areas to see improvement? Make one practical change prior to our next session.

3. From this biblical narrative we see that God is comforter and sustainer. Take some time to reflect on these attributes of who God is and write out a prayer asking God to comfort and sustain you. Close the prayer with specific points of thanksgiving for God and who he is.

2 CHRONICLES
18

HEART ALLEGIANCE & PEER CONFORMITY

By: Jay Younts

www.Everydaytalk247.com

Back Story: Jehoshaphat & Ahab

- 2 Chronicles 17–20 tells the story of Jehoshaphat, son of Asa and the fourth king of Judah who lived in the 9th century B.C. Jehoshaphat is an example of God's faithfulness even when we are stupid.

- As Chapter 17 indicates, Jehoshaphat began his reign by ruling well.

- However, in Chapter 18 he makes critical errors in judgment based on a toxic shift in the allegiance of his heart.

IN SESSION COUNSELING

Have your counselee read 2 Chronicles Chapter 18 aloud, and then together discuss the following observations and questions.

- After knowing God's blessing, Jehoshaphat aligns himself with Ahab by marriage. He goes to celebrate with Ahab. Then, Ahab, king of Israel, asked Jehoshaphat king of Judah, "Will you go with me against Ramoth Gilead?"
- How did Jehoshaphat respond? His heart allegiance shifted by replying "I am as you are, and my people as your people; we will join you in the war (vs. 3)."
- What changed in Jehoshaphat's thinking to bring about this shift and caving into peer conformity?
  » *Perhaps Jehoshaphat was attracted by Ahab's reputation as a great warrior –*
  » *Perhaps he wanted to add to his wealth or protect Judah by political alliance*
  » *Perhaps he was taken in by flattery and praise - Proverbs 27:6*
  » *Perhaps he was attracted by the party scene and sexual temptation of the northern kingdom*
  » *Perhaps he was naïve about Ahab's manipulation.*

- Whatever the reason, Jehoshaphat obligates himself to go to war. He declares himself to be one with God's enemy. In verse 4 Jehoshaphat makes the right request but his heart is already compromised! Several indicators in the story show that even when Jehoshaphat makes a correct assessment his heart is aligned with Ahab and not with God.

Takeaway:

The wrong heart allegiance will diminish our ability to have discernment. We will be stupid. We won't recognize the warning signs of danger. We will see things going from bad to worse and won't be able to stop it, because we don't know why – just like Jehoshaphat.

- Notice Micaiah's response in contrast to Jehoshaphat's. Micaiah's heart allegiance is solid. He is not swayed by circumstances. See verses 12–27.
- Even with Micaiah's example and clear warning, Jehoshaphat still is clueless: evidence of a misguided heart.

- Verse 29 reveals Ahab's plan in which Jehoshaphat is to play the fool to protect Ahab!
- Jehoshaphat agrees to Ahab's plan!! Think about this, the definition of stupidity. Sin makes you stupid.
- When the chariot commanders saw Jehoshaphat, they thought, "This is the king of Israel." So, they turned to attack him, but Jehoshaphat cried out, and the Lord rescued him.

Takeaway:

This is why heart allegiance matters. God does not love us because we do everything right. There is hope when we do stupid things! He loves us even when we are stupid. He loves us because Jesus died for us. We can always cry out even when things look like there is no hope. When peer pressure and peer conformity is an issue we always want to check for the issues regarding heart allegiance. This will provide us with insight and discernment as to why we do things we know we will regret.

AFTER SESSION ASSIGNMENT

This week go back and read 2 Chronicles 18 again. Journal your answers to the questions below and bring back to our counseling session next week to discuss.

1. Who and what are the Ahabs in your life?

2. How should have Jehoshaphat responded?

3. When did Jehoshaphat get in trouble?

4. Why would Jehoshaphat ignore the clear teaching of God (v.3)?

JOB 1

SUFFERING IS ABOUT MORE THAN SANCTIFICATION

By: Betty-Anne Van Rees

www.biblicalcounselingcanada.ca

Job's story is so disturbing that we are inclined to look away. It's more than we can take in — or want to take in. Though righteous, he suffered profoundly: layer upon layer of grief, trauma upon trauma. Everything … almost everyone gone. How are we to think about suffering in light of Job's experience?

IN SESSION COUNSELING
Read Job 1:6–12 aloud and discuss the following questions.

What do we learn about the man, Job?
- He was unlike any man on earth: "blameless and upright, fearing God and turning away from evil." Satan believed him to be protected by God.

How did Job's suffering come about?
- God drew Satan's attention to Job.
- Satan asked permission of God and God granted that permission.

Teaching Point:
Job did not face his trial because God "needed to fix him."

Read Job 1:13–22

How did Job respond to his suffering and loss?
- In humble faith in God's sovereign hand, he accepted what God has chosen for him and worshipped.

As suffering lingered, we learn in future chapters how Job's response changed.
- 3:1 - "I wish the day I was born had never happened."
- 7:2–6 - The suffering is overwhelming, clouding his view of God.
- 7:20 - Why have you made me your mark (target)?

Teaching Point:
A faith response does not negate grief and confusion.

God speaks
- Chapters 38–41 - It is as if God takes Job by the chin and says, "Look at me. Remember who I am. Remember my supremacy, my intimate care of my creation. I see you."

Teaching Point:
God may not answer the questions you are asking, but if you are listening, He is speaking the answers you need.

Job responds to God
- 42:2 - I hear you. "You can do all things and no purpose of yours can be thwarted."
- 42:3 - In response to God in 38:2, "I am the one who uttered what I did not understand."
- 42:5 - "I had heard of you by the hearing of the ear, but now my eye sees you." This is the climax of Job's story.

Teaching Point:
Job knew about God before, but his suffering, and his struggle in his suffering brought him to a new place of intimacy with God. The nature of the statement conveys how highly valuable this was to him. This new knowledge humbles him (v. 6).

AFTER SESSION ASSIGNMENT

1. In writing, honestly lay your sorrows and questions before God. Tell him what is hard and how you are feeling about your current suffering. What do you believe about why you are suffering?

2. 2 Cor 3:18: "And we all, with unveiled face, beholding the glory of the Lord, are being transformed into the same image from one degree of glory to another. For this comes from the Lord who is the Spirit." Note God's process of change in this verse. We change the more we are "seeing" God. Be intentional every day in the next week about looking for God — in His word and in His world (Ps. 19). Look long enough until you are moved to worship. Note how you have seen Him.

3. Is anything hindering you from moving toward Jesus in courageous faith that trusts His sovereign hand and relies on Him without reservation? What fears, doubts or questions move you to try to keep him at a distance? Be prepared to share these the next time we meet.

NOTES

JOB 9

WHEN GOD SEEMS SILENT IN OUR SUFFERING

By: Jonathan D. Holmes
www.fieldstonecounseling.org

JOB 9

The book of Job is one of the earliest books in the Bible chronologically (even though it's toward the middle of the OT). In this book, we learn about the man Job, the reality of human suffering, and the heartache and pain of friends who hurt more than help. Through it all, Job maintains his faith and cries out to God. In the end he gets a surprising response from God that sheds little light on the *why* of his suffering, but instead points him to the *who* in the midst of his suffering.

IN SESSION COUNSELING

Read Job 9:1–35 together, alternating every other verse between counselor and counselee.

Q1: Describe your visceral and instinctive reaction to what you read. Where do you identify with Job and his situation? What feels different?

Q2: Back up and read Bildad's counsel to Job in Job 8:2–7. What are some of the hurtful and unhelpful things people have said to you in your suffering?

Q3: Make a list of questions you have of God right now in your situation. Where do you feel unheard or misunderstood by God or others?

Throughout Job 9, Job honestly cries out to God about his situation. He describes some of the ways he feels God is treating him/dealing with him. Make a list of these experiences–

Vs. 3:

Vs. 11:

Vs. 13–14:

Vs. 15–18:

Vs. 32–35:

AFTER SESSION ASSIGNMENT

In verses 27–31, Job lists several things he could try to do in order to alleviate his suffering and be in a right relationship before God. What are some things you have done to try and alleviate and relieve your suffering?

In verse 33, Job identifies the main problem as he sees it. In your own words explain Job 9:33. How does Jesus Christ address and fulfill Job's conundrum here?

Read Isaiah 53:3–5. What comfort can be found in Jesus being identified as a "man of sorrows, and acquainted with grief"?

Write out a similar lament to God as Job did in chapter 9. Include some of the elements Job included here. In what ways might your lament end on a more hopeful note than Job's?

PSALM 1

SIMPLE FAITH

By: Margaret Ashmore
www.margaretashmore.com

PSALM 1

St. Jerome of the 5th century called Psalm 1 *"the handbook on the whole of the bible"* because it puts before the reader two clear choices: joy or depression, God or the world, truth or lies. The problems of the human soul can be complicated but God's answer never is.

The apostle Paul said, *"But I fear, lest by any means, as the serpent beguiled Eve through his subtilty, so your minds should be corrupted from the simplicity that is in Christ."* (2 Cor. 11:3) It is Satan's policy to complicate scripture and corrupt minds. Therefore, it is for those who counsel with God's Word to be straightforward and honest, not trying to spare feelings but to spur faithfulness leading to restoration. Psalm 1 is the handbook, calling the counselee back to personal responsibility. The choices are simple. The question is, will we obey?

IN SESSION COUNSELING
Read Psalm 1 and discuss the following three questions:

What do we learn about living a blessed life?
*   There are three things to avoid (worldly counsel, courses, and company) and one thing to do: meditate on the Word of God. Profoundly simple.

*   God stands at the crossroads of every life pointing out the way of blessedness, "the happy condition of those who love the Lord and keep His commandments." Will we go His way or the way of the world? It is a choice.

What are the three things God is telling us to avoid?
*   First, worldly counsel. The word counsel in this text means to influence and convince. It is beguiling to listen to worldly counsel (adopted by Freud's "ethic of non-responsibility") that says "it is not your fault." Which is why the very first warning is the most important: we are being admonished to guard with all diligence against what appears to be the right counsel but is instead, deceitful. John Calvin said: "The psalmist begins with COUNSEL, by which term I understand the wickedness which does not as yet show itself openly."

*   Second and third, listening to the world will put us on the path of the worldly which leads to destruction. (Proverbs 4:14–15) The influence deepens until we now find ourselves hardened and proud, seeing ourselves as the arbiter of what we determine to be true while scoffing at The Truth. (Romans 1:18–23)

*   We are no longer malleable to change. Like Jonah, we now have to "hit bottom" in order to cry out to God.

What is the one thing to do?
*   Mortification (the three negatives) now leads to enlivened soil so that we can "receive the Word implanted which is able to save our souls." (James 1:21)

- We now can identity the lies and replace them with the Truth and as such, we will be set free. (John 8:32)

- A good practice is to list the lies that tend to rule our hearts and then meditate on the truth of God's Word which will overtake them like the sunrise overtakes the darkness.

AFTER SESSION ASSIGNMENT

1. Be very purposeful in writing down the lies from worldly counsel and counter them with a specific verse. Mediate on that verse until the lies dissipate and the truth fills, heals, and seals you in and with the love of Christ.

2. Begin to take personal responsibility instead of blaming. Call sin, "sin" and not a mistake or a disorder. According to Psalm 32, you will shout for joy!

PSALM 16

UNSHAKEABLE FAITH

By: Shanda Anderson
www.austinstonecounseling.org

Living in a world of famine and sorrow we set our eyes on the future grace of eternity, "where all sad things will come untrue" (Tolkien). Our weary and hungry souls find daily refuge and fullness in the presence of our loving God who journeys with us. Like David, we will need to remind ourselves of the light of God's counsel and the goodness of His character during times of doubt and discouragement. Psalm 16 reminds us of the resurrection and gives us good evidence and encouragement to walk the narrow path of life, following our suffering and risen Savior. Because Jesus did not see corruption and defeated death, we can endure the challenges of life with an unshakable faith that rejoices in the security and pleasure found in Him.

IN SESSION COUNSELING

1. **Acknowledge Your Need**
   The Psalmist humbly admits his desperate need for God's provision. There's no leaning into self-reliance or self-sufficiency. He knows there is only one place where hope resides and refuses to turn aside and seek help anywhere else. There is no shame in honestly admitting our immutable need for God's provision and rescue. God can handle our weakness and often uses it to show just how present, powerful, and caring He is.

2. **See Your Inheritance**
   In the first 8 verses of Psalm 16 David transitions from "Preserve me, O God" in verse 1 to "I will not be shaken" in verse 8. What truth did David encounter that turned his heart and mind to such confidence and assurance? What promises of God produced a galvanized proclamation of faith and gladness heart, security, delight, confidence, and fullness of joy? Looking with David into the treasures of our present and future inheritance will bring hope and deep satisfaction to our weary soul which has been bombarded and burdened by a broken humanity and sin-sick world. There is power in His counsel and safety in His design for the soul that looks to Him who sovereignly reigns and rules over every detail of His unfolding story.

3. **See Your Savior**
   When navigating suffering and unbelief, the fearful heart of man can become glad and dwell secure. Fixing our eyes upon Jesus, the hope that will not disappoint, invigorates and refreshes the weary soul that feels temptation to lose heart. Remembering the One who rescued and ransomed us while we were sinners brings gratitude for this gift of forgiveness and reconciliation, restoring our worship and directing our attention to the glory of our good Father in Heaven. No place or person will ever offer the security or pleasure that is found in Christ. May we find deep satisfaction and sweet delight in Him.

AFTER SESSION ASSIGNMENT

1. In what places, other than God, have you sought to find refuge? How have you taken refuge in God this week? If you are struggling to find your greatest security and refuge in God, what is one practical step you can take toward leaning into Him when you are fearful and discouraged? v. 1–3

2. What are you running after that is multiplying your sorrow? Consider the benefit of holiness and purity that is meant to protect and guard you from the effects of sin. What practical step can you take to direct your heart to say "yes" to God and orient your life to His loving and good commands? v. 4

3. Where do you feel like God is withholding something from you? What would change if you believed that every detail of your life is carefully directed by the Creator of the world and that His plan for you and your life is good? List the ways you are able to see God currently providing for you in practical ways. List some of the promises God has eternally offered to you as a future inheritance. Meditate on all that He has for you and ponder His kindness that gives good gifts. v. 5–6

4. What gets in the way of you remembering to ask God for help? What distractions hinder you from meditating on Scripture so you can call to mind His wisdom when you need guidance? What fears arise as you consider making Christ your highest and greatest treasure? v. 7–11

5. Read the message from John Piper on Psalm 16 *www.desiringgod.org/messages/the-path-to-full-and-lasting-pleasure* and write out the points that most impact you.

PSALM51

TRUE REPENTANCE

By: Lee Lewis
www.soulcareconsulting.com

PSALM 51

Psalm 51 is a response from King David to God after the prophet Nathan confronts him over his sins in 2 Samuel 11–12. David's broken and heart-filled response to the Lord gives us a clear picture of what true repentance looks like. This psalm teaches us that God's grace is sometimes violent in order to break us away from sin and bondage. True repentance is absolutely necessary in order for healing and cleansing to take place.

IN SESSION COUNSELING

Read Psalm 51 aloud and discuss the following questions.

Where does mercy for David's sins come from?

- David cannot appeal to merit, the law, or morals. True repentance confesses guilt and doesn't base hope for forgiveness on our own deeds. No self-atonement can cleanse our sins. If God has mercy, it is only through his good grace and choosing.

- True repentance recognizes that mercy comes from God to those who see their sin/iniquities before a holy God. David takes full responsibility. He doesn't blame, sidestep, or justify his actions.

What does David's confession entail?

- Against You I have sinned (v. 4) – He sees his sin before a holy God first and foremost. This is a direct contrast to his actions in 2 Samuel 11 where his efforts are totally self-absorbed in seeking to cover his sins. David's response in Psalm 51:4 is in essence saying, "How could I treat God like this?"

- Blameless in your judgement (v. 4b) – We deserve whatever punishment the Lord decides to bring. This statement by David rightly sees that he deserves nothing but God's just justice. It is similar to the thief on the cross in Luke 23:41 acknowledging Jesus as the Christ. The thief says, "We are receiving due rewards for our deeds."

- Brought forth in iniquity (v. 5) – David speaks to original sin and human depravity. He is further speaking to what is said in verse 3, that our sin is ever before us. This speaks to what most affects and ails our lives, and that is our sinful hearts.

- Inward being & secret heart (v. 6) – The heart/soul is the epicenter from which worship and affections flow. True confession and repentance are deeply spiritual and recognizes that our deepest need for healing and cleansing is derived from the heart. And only God can cleanse and change our hearts.

What do we learn about God?

- Only God can cleanse our sins and what he cleanses is clean. His cleansing work goes all the way to the source. He cleanses our hearts.

- The Lord loves us enough to expose our sins. This feels horrifying, but it is his grace to not leave us in our sin and hiding. The Lord brings conviction because he wants restoration and reconciliation.

- God draws near to the broken spirit and contrite heart. He is opposed to our pride, but draws near to cleanse those who are humble, needy, and asking for his help.

How does Psalm 51 point to the Gospel?

- Verses 16 and 17 speak to the Old Testament ceremonies of blood offerings and sacrifices for sins. Without sorrow for sin no blood offered would even matter. This is where the Gospel is seen so clearly. Hebrews 10:5–10 speaks to this exact statement in that Jesus Christ is the once and for all offering that saves, cleanses, and sanctifies us from sin and death. True repentance is brought to the unmistaken reality that it is through Christ alone that we find cleansing and forgiveness from our sins. God has made a way through Christ for us to be cleansed and reconciled to himself.

AFTER SESSION ASSIGNMENT

1. Read Luke 18:9–14, Luke 15:18–21, Luke 23:41, Matthew 23:25–28, and Hebrews 10:5–10. How do these references line up with Psalm 51?

2. True repentance has three elements: an accurate view of sin, an accurate view of God, and an accurate view of self. Which aspect(s) do you need to grow in?

PSALM 77

PERSEVERING FAITH

By: Shanda Anderson
www.austinstonecounseling.org

Sometimes, perseverance looks gritty and raw. There are moments in our faith where we find ourselves wrestling with God as the only way we know how to draw near to Him. We often want to appear refined and elegant as we bow down to God's commands, but many moments in the Christian life are marked by our feeble and messy efforts to stay in the tensions of the story God is authoring. Jacob grappled with God as he held on and refused to let go, no matter how much weariness and hopelessness were enticing him to give up. Our daring interactions with God in the midst of unwanted circumstances can become a sacred ground of increased trust if we learn from this psalm where to look when hope seems dim. Psalm 77 invites the sorrowful soul to pour out all of the questions and doubts to God, and then consider God's faithfulness throughout time and history as a gentle and steady whisper to the parched soul. Some of the boldest questions toward God emerge from this psalmist who feels defeated and overwhelmed in the first 10 verses. Then, something happens, a shift, a change of thought and an adjusted heart focus. Sometimes, we must pull back from our own life and felt experience to remember the unyielding and active redemptive faithfulness of God even when we can't see it.

IN SESSION COUNSELING

1. **Lament is a form of worship.**

   There are six questions in verses 7–9 that will make you uncomfortable, if you are honest. This psalmist cries out, seeks, remembers, meditates, considers, and waits for God. Although good spiritual disciplines and practices were applied, the psalmist says… "my soul refuses to be comforted, I am so troubled I cannot speak; when I remember God, I moan; when I meditate, my spirit faints." Hope seems out of reach and sorrow swallows every effort to gain perspective. How reassuring it is to know that we can bring our broken heart and discouraged soul to the Father of all comfort. Complaints brought to God can be transformed into worship as we lift our eyes beyond our situational pain to consider His undeniable faithfulness to His people.

2. **Felt experience is to be acknowledged but should not be allowed to determine next steps.**

   Our bodies will feel the weight of grief and sorrow. Swirling doubts will invade our mind and tempt us to view God through a darkened and foggy lens of suffering. We will lose sight of the God of our salvation when times of anguish and deep pain seem to distort every attempt to move towards seeing God as good. We can validate the challenge and discomfort of our emotions, but we will need to look to the historical activity of God throughout the ages to guide our worship through the gauntlet of grief. Psalm 77:10–20 shows us what it looks like to admit our pain but be led by God's redemptive glory that outweighs our doubts and limited point of view.

3. **God's character and His love is not determined by our circumstances.**

   There came a time in this psalmist's wrestling where a deliberate choice was made to look beyond the current emotional climate and landscape of life difficulty. As we live life in this broken world stained with sin, our senses that will help us connect to

God and find delight in God may work one day and then fail us the next. We need not be surprised that the measures and methods that work to bring encouragement and cleared vision in one area of struggle may cease to give way to the same outcome when applied again to a different agonizing trial. Although the approach will vary and the outcome will fluctuate, the character of God is fixed, unchanging, steady, reliable, and consistent. Like a gyroscope with a fixed axis that always knows true north in order to navigate uncertain waters, so is the steadfast character of God an anchor to hold us when the stormy seas of life are choppy and rough.

AFTER SESSION ASSIGNMENT

1. How do you relate to the Psalmist?

2. Where does your focus need to shift in your life and felt experience to remember the unyielding and active redemptive faithfulness of God?

3. Write your own lament and allow God to direct your attention to His faithfulness throughout your life and history beyond your life.

4. Read "Dark Clouds, Deep Mercy" by Mark Vroegop and spend some time considering the questions at the end of each chapter.

ISAIAH 49

TRUSTING GOD FOR OUR REWARD

By: Jeremy Lelek, Ph.D.
www.christiancounseling.com

Counseling can often be a journey of patience and perseverance. Applying biblical truth is not a silver bullet that instantly alleviates depression or anxiety, nor does it instantaneously heal broken marriages. It takes humble hearts obediently submitting to God's Word in faith that his promises are sure. Sometimes when the process of change comes slow, individuals and couples can become discouraged and despondent. The work can often feel futile. The good news is that Jesus understands this experience, and provides a wonderful image of persevering in the process. The book of Isaiah provides us with one of the most vivid examples of our Lord pressing in while experiencing a sense that his works were in vain.

IN SESSION COUNSELING
Read Isaiah 49:1–5

This passage is referring to Jesus being eternally prepared for the work He would do on earth (v. 1–3)

In verse four we read Jesus' response to the Father. Several striking things stand out:
- Jesus felt his ministry was in vain.
- Jesus felt he had spent his strength for nothing and vanity.

Have you experienced this in the counseling process or in your current struggle (or chronic struggles)?
- Jesus moves toward you in your discouragement.
- Jesus understands, and His heart is moved.

The second half of verse four illustrates the faithfulness and perfection of Jesus in the midst of extreme pain.
- Jesus exhibits perfect faith.
- His reward is in the hands of God.

In your own struggle with discouragement or doubt:
- Move toward Jesus with a heart of gratitude in that in his own sense of purposelessness he continued to exhibit perfect faith, and that perfection is now yours in your union with Him.
- Be encouraged that Jesus knew in your suffering you might not always "get it right." He knows suffering well, and willingly submitted to these experiences as a result that he might be our merciful and faithful high priest (Heb. 2:17).

Read Isaiah 49:6

Notice the heart of the Father toward the Son. He reveals to the Son the reward that would come from his work on earth. It wouldn't impact just one small nation, but it would CHANGE the world!
- In our union with Jesus, the Father's heart toward you is the same as His heart toward His only begotten Son.
- While persevering in patience (and maybe feeling discouraged), be reminded that God's purposes in this trial are perfect and beautiful. Just as He was immensely

faithful to Jesus in his trial in bringing perfect and abundant reward, so it will he be with you.

AFTER SESSION ASSIGNMENT

1. Reread the passages for this exercise. Imagine how difficult things had to be for Jesus to feel purposeless in his life and ministry.

2. Read Matthew 26:38–42. Meditate on Jesus' sorrow and His faithfulness in his mission to persevere because He loved you.

3. Write out a prayer of gratitude to Jesus for his faithfulness to persevere in the midst of pain and feelings of vanity.

4. Consider how He will also be faithful to you in your current situation.

JEREMIAH 3

BROKEN CISTERNS

By: Jesse Pirkle
www.sohillscc.com

Jeremiah, who is also known as the "weeping prophet," served as a prophet to Judah during some of the most difficult seasons recorded in Scripture. The nation was forsaking the Lord and turning to idols. Although the Lord sent reminders of His goodness and longed for the faithfulness of Judah, the people would not listen. Jeremiah consistently pleaded with Judah to repent—warning them of the coming judgement of God. In Jeremiah 2, the Lord uses unforgettable imagery to define Judah's idolatry.

IN SESSION COUNSELING
Read Jeremiah 2:11–13 aloud and discuss the following questions.

What is idolatry?
- Idolatry is simply worshipping something other than the one, true God. Every person was created to worship God and is a worshipper by nature. The question is never, "Do we worship?" but "What do we worship?".

- Here in Jeremiah, Judah's idolatry is symbolized by two different sources for water: the fountain of living waters (the Lord) and broken cisterns (the false gods/idols). Judah has turned to the broken cisterns.

- Idolatry is committing two sins; Forsaking God and going somewhere other than God as a source of fulfillment.

- In the book Gospel Treason, Brad defines idolatry as "Anything or Anyone that begins to Capture our Hearts and Minds and Affections more than God".

What might idols look like today?
- Read Colossians 3:5. Although we may not be physically bowing before a wooden statue or vowing to worship a false god, Paul says that evil thoughts, desires, and actions signify idolatry.

- Anytime we put our own desires on a pedestal and choose our way over God's, we are becoming self-worshippers. We are, in essence, turning to the broken cistern of self.

- Idolatry is usually composed of both an idolatrous desire and an object (broken cistern) where we go to get the desire met/fulfilled. Example; Alcohol (object) for comfort or escape (desire), Spouse (object) for happiness or approval (desire).

- Where have you forsaken God as the source of fulfillment in your desires for Security (protection from some form of hardship), Affection (love), Meaning/Purpose (who am I), Satisfaction, Happiness (Joy), Approval, Acceptance, Comfort, Refuge, Escape, Strength, Pleasure, Success, etc.

What is the result of unrepentant idolatry?
- Judgment and the wrath of God are the result. Jeremiah warns Judah again and again of what will happen because of idolatry. Judah refuses to listen and ultimately, the Israelites are taken as captives in Babylon. Similarly, in Colossians 3:6, Paul warns that "on account of these the wrath of God is coming."

- A life of constant thirst results. When we aren't satisfied with the Fountain of Living Water, we will turn again and again to what we think will satisfy us. The Lord, in His love and wisdom, tells us that idolatry is a broken cistern: it will not and cannot satisfy you.

- Idolatry is breaking Commandments 1 and 2. Read Deuteronomy 5: 7-9. Seek to identify the ungodly masters, functional gods, that occupy positions of authority in your heart. What or whom is controlling your actions, thoughts, emotions, and attitudes?

AFTER SESSION ASSIGNMENT

1. What have you learned as we've discussed idolatry? In what way(s) are you tempted to forsake the Lord and turn to your own way?

2. Read Colossians 3. In Christ, you can change. With God's Word and Spirit, you can "put to death what is earthly in you." From this chapter, what do you need to "put off"? And what do you need to "put on"?

3. Listen to a sermon from John Piper, titled "The Ultimate Essence of Evil" and journal your response to the sermon. In your life, how have you seen that sin cannot satisfy your soul?

4. Journal your responses to these questions and bring back to our next session for discussion. What do you think you "must have" in order to be satisfied/happy/fulfilled outside of Christ alone? Are you willing to sin to get it? Are you willing to sin if you don't get it?

5. What do you need to ask God to forgive you for concerning the two sins in Jeremiah 2:11-13?
   a. Forsaking God as the source of _ABC__ (desire)
   b. Going to _____XYZ_____ (object of desire) to get the above desire filled.
   c. Identify your idolatrous desire and confess it to God by filling in the blanks:
   Lord, please forgive me for forsaking You and going to _____ to be the source of _____ for me. Please help me not to do this, but rather to choose to be intentional in every moment to remember Your Truth and then think and act according to it with the help of the Holy Spirit."

LAMENTATIONS 3

BUT THIS I CALL TO MIND...

By: Jeremy Lelek, Ph.D.
www.metroplexcounseling.com

LAMENTATIONS 3

Lamentations is a series of reflections by the prophet Jeremiah following the destruction of Israel. The ache and agony of his broken heart are palpable as he witnesses God's justice "thrown down without pity" (Lam. 2:17). The prophet discloses his own vulnerable emotional state citing profound distress, a churning stomach, and a heart that was wrung (Lam. 1:20). This exercise will hone its focus on chapter 3 of Lamentations while considering the impact of one's thoughts and beliefs on perspective and lived experience.

IN SESSION COUNSELING

Read Lamentations 3:1–33 and then consider the questions below.

List five ways that Jeremiah describes God and his own suffering in the first nineteen verses (ex. "He is a bear lying in wait for me")

1.

2.

3.

4.

5.

Describe Jeremiah's lived experience in verses 17–20 when conceptualizing God this way.

What gave Jeremiah hope in verses 21–24? Did his situation change or did his beliefs about God and his situation change?

List five ways Jeremiah describes his situation and suffering after his views of God are transformed (see verses 23–39). Discuss the differences in these five statements compared to the list in question one above.

1.

2.

3.

4.

5.

AFTER SESSION ASSIGNMENT

1. Write out your gut level beliefs about your current situation. Do these correspond with a loving, caring, and merciful God?

2. Write out a new set of beliefs about your situation that would correspond with a loving, caring, and merciful God.

3. Read and journal on Lamentations 3:21–24. Recall times in your life when you have experienced God's love, care, and mercy.

4. Pray a prayer of earnest gratitude for those moments when God's love, care, and mercy were experienced.

EZEKIEL 37 1-14

THE GOD WHO RAISES THE DEAD

By: Susan Thomas
www.passionatelife.com

In this life-changing narrative, we see the power of God to bring dry bones back to life. As we step into this moment of the priest and prophet Ezekiel, we witness his encounter with the God who raises the dead. As God asks Ezekiel probing questions and then commands him to speak God's word in faith, we can almost hear the sounds of dry bones rattling and the gasp of breath as bodies breathe again. God is still in the business of raising the dead. Even when it feels like hope is lost, with Christ we have HOPE.

IN SESSION COUNSELING
Read Ezekiel 37:1–14 and discuss the following questions.

Discuss what is happening in this passage and how it might apply to us.
* God takes Ezekiel to a valley full of dead, dry bones. God asks him an impossible question: "Can these bones become living people again?"

* We see God do what only God can do. God breathes life into dead people. What was once a pile of dry bones is now an army prepared for victory.

* "When this happens, O my people, you will know that I am the Lord (v.13)."

* What seemingly impossible or hopeless situation are you facing in your life right now?

Lessons from the Dry Bones
* There is no situation that is impossible for God.

* As God engaged Ezekiel, God wants to engage us in our darkest valley or dead place.

* Ezekiel's faith was demonstrated as he obeyed God and "spoke the message as he commanded..." His faith was rewarded with the miracle of seeing dry bones come to life!

* There is power when we believe and speak God's word over our lives and situations.

* There is blessing and reward when we obey God and follow Him.

* God alone can breathe life into dead things. We can trust Him.

How does this narrative point to Jesus?
* All of the Bible points to the Good News of Jesus Christ, our Savior and Lord.

* Ultimately God sent Jesus to die for our sins and conquer death so we can now live. (Read Romans 6:6–11.)

* For us who place our faith in Christ, God resurrects our souls for all eternity. As we trust and follow Him daily, we will witness God resurrect the "dead places" in our lives here and now.

EZEKIEL 37:1-14

AFTER SESSION ASSIGNMENT

Re-read Ezekiel 37:1–14 and ask the Holy Spirit to help you trust and obey God's Word.

What are some "dead places" in your life right now? (i.e., relational, emotional, etc.)

What keeps you from believing God in your situation?

What are some promises of God that you can believe and pray (out loud) over your dead places? (i.e, Read and pray Philippians 4:13.)

Pray:

"God please help me believe you even for the most difficult places in my life. When I struggle with my faith, help my unbelief. I declare that you are the God who raises the dead. Because of Jesus, that same power is available to me and my life today. In Jesus' name, Amen."

DANIEL 2

FROM WHOM COME JUDGMENT AND PRESERVATION

By: John Henderson
www.christiancounseling.com

What burdens us? More importantly, upon whom and what do we depend when our circumstances crumble? When the foundations are destroyed, what can the righteous do? What can you believe and do? In the book of Daniel, chapters 2–4, we find the answer to this question by helping us see how to anchor our thoughts and affections in God, to center our view of the world around Jesus Christ, and to fix our faith upon the One from whom we receive wisdom and might, through whom comes deliverance, and to whom belongs the kingdom. In this narrative we learn that, *in whatever trials we face, let us seek and cry out to God through Jesus Christ, who supplies wisdom and might as we trust and follow Him.*

IN SESSION COUNSELING
Read Daniel 2:1–16:
Think through the following questions as you help guide your counselee through the narrative.
- What is Nebuchadnezzar in need of?
- What happens to someone if they can't interpret the dream?
- Does this situation seem possible for any human to do what the king requires?
- What characteristics do you see in Daniel by his response?

Read Daniel 2:17–30:
Discuss the points below and take time to help your counselee reflect on their own situation.

Daniel was under the threat of death unless he received wisdom from God for knowing and interpreting Nebuchadnezzar's dream, strength to face the king, declare it boldly, and endure whatever came next. In Daniel's response he doesn't panic, collapse in despair or just give up at the hopelessness of the situation. He prays. He calls upon his friends to pray. In praying and asking others to pray, Daniel knows this is an opportunity for the wisdom and power of God to be displayed, and He knows that's what he needs: not a new circumstance, but a great God to show up.
- How many of our prayers, if answered, would result in a more glorious circumstance, and a less glorified God?
- What are you facing right now that requires deeper wisdom and greater strength than you possess?
- How can your prayer life change so that when you face trials of any kind, you know that in such moments you need to learn how to have dependence upon God, and how to cry out for wisdom, and how to trust He will through Christ deliver you in His time and in His way and for His glory?

God revealed to Daniel Nebuchadnezzar's dream and its interpretation while Daniel slept. Daniel worships. What he declares about God through these words of praise is life changing and life giving. The truth revealed through his words should be the foundation of our faith and hope every day, but especially in days of trouble.
- Think about how much of your life and how many circumstances in your life come down to needing understanding from God about how to rightly interpret the situation and rightly respond (wisdom) and needing strength from God to endure trials and temptations (might).

DANIEL 2

Read Daniel 2:31–49:

Daniel interprets the dream. The Lord uses Daniel, not only to reveal the mystery, but to reveal the God who reveals mysteries and His sovereign power over history, and Nebuchadnezzar will be astounded; still ignorant, but astounded nonetheless.

The wisdom Daniel receives is this: God knows what He's doing; God is sovereign over everything; He changes the seasons; He gives dreams to kings and robs them of their sleep; God reveals mysteries to whom He wills. God brings about what He reveals in dreams; God is moving history according to His perfect will; God is glorifying Himself through these events; God is redeeming His people through all these events; a King and kingdom are coming to which every earthly king and kingdom are mere copies and signs; The Lord's Christ is coming to deliver and reign; everything is from Him and through Him and to Him. If we seek first His kingdom and love Him above all, we will understand how to live in our present-day circumstances.

The might Daniel receives is this: The God he serves is with him and in control, so he's strengthened to be faithful; the God he serves in near and good, so with His strength he can endure affliction; the King he serves is the true King, so he can be encouraged when suffering; the kingdom to which he belongs is an everlasting kingdom, so he can persevere until the end. It's not hopeless. It's not pointless. It's not out of control. God hears his prayers. God makes known what Daniel asked of Him, but even more. Through Daniel the Lord will proclaim His glory and power. Through Daniel the Lord will preach good news. Through little Daniel, trapped inside this big Babylon, the Lord will bring about His mighty kingdom.

Daniel got a glimpse of all this through the interpretation of a dream God gave to an unbelieving king. How much more have we been given through His Word, through the gospel, through the Christ who has been revealed as the wisdom and power of God. And then in these days He sent forth His Christ to redeem His people and establish a kingdom that will never fail, and allows us to share in that kingdom with Him. That's the grand work of God of which we are part.

If He's doing that for us, then how much more will He help us understand and endure every trial in this life? It's going to be okay. We don't need to control everything. We pray. We don't need to avoid trouble. We face it with Him. We don't need to worry about how we're going to get there. We just need to trust and follow Jesus.

AFTER SESSION ASSIGNMENT
Reread Daniel chapter two and continue reflecting on the questions we discussed today. Journal as the Lord reveals new things to you.

DANIEL 3

THROUGH WHOM COMES DELIVERANCE

By: John Henderson
www.biblicalcc.org

Life can be full of those kinds of moments when the Lord mercifully rescues us from momentary trials and then uses such times to make a bigger point: He is our Deliverer. And someday He will deliver us from every peril, from our enemies, from our sin, and most importantly, from His wrath. The Bible reveals these truths repeatedly, and Daniel 3 is one of those places. Through the story of three men, sentenced to being burned to death for refusing to bow to an idol, the Lord reveals that He stands with His people in their trials and that He can deliver them, thereby proving that He alone can deliver them from the fires of judgment to come. Through this narrative we learn that, *when facing trials of this life, let us entrust ourselves to God through Jesus Christ, who walks with us in this present life and delivers us from the wrath to come.*

IN SESSION COUNSELING
Read Daniel 3:1–30:
Discuss the points below and take time to help your counselee reflect on their own situation.

Though God intends to gather for Himself a people from every tribe and tongue to worship and enjoy Him forever, Nebuchadnezzar has a different plan: to gather all peoples, nations, and languages to worship his idol. So, Nebuchadnezzar orders everyone to bow and wanted the people to worship his idol (worshipping something or someone other than God).

- What kind of idols do we have today? What specific idols do you struggle with?

No matter how discretely we might try to express our faithfulness to Jesus, He will allow Satan to stir up malicious opponents who call attention to our faith and accuse us of wrongdoing, who use human laws to wage spiritual war. Shadrach, Meshach, and Abednego openly refuse to bow. They openly stand in devotion to the Lord their God and accept the cost. It may look as though Nebuchadnezzar is calling all the shots, but no, God is moving every piece around the table in order to bring the whole account to that question. *"Who is the god who will deliver you out of my hands?"* As far as Nebuchadnezzar is concerned, there are no hands greater than his own. He demands their fear. The threat is persecution and death for their faith. For you and me ... well ... it could be anything. Who will deliver you from abuse? Who will deliver you from cancer? Who will deliver you from the hardships of this life? Who will deliver you from the sins that entangle you?

- What seems to be throwing this question out at you? Satan, an addiction, an eating disorder, an enslaving sin, a physical affliction?

Deliverance is our great need. Shadrach, Meshach, and Abednego realize that this question is primarily about God, not us. Their situation is about God's glory and power. Their moment of truth is about trusting in Him to care for them. Their trial by fire is about making Him known and courageously accepting the consequences. Their acceptance of the Lord's love for them does not mean He will keep them from being thrown into a furnace. These men knew and trusted God. They said, *He is able ... He will deliver us* because that is who He is, a redeeming God. The power of the king is irrelevant. The accusations of the opponents, the size of their army, or even the temperature of the furnace, as we will see, counts for nothing. As the narrative continues we see that the fire did not leave a mark, not even a smell. Incredible! God proved their faith to be rightly placed in Him. Even Nebuchadnezzar pronounces, *"There is no other god who is able to rescue in this way."*

•   How does their faith and trust in God bring encouragement into your situation?

AFTER SESSION ASSIGNMENT
Reread Daniel chapter three and continue reflecting on the questions we discussed today. Journal as the Lord reveals new things to you.

God the Father sent God the Son to walk in the fire we deserve, to cover us in His righteousness so that we can survive the Day of Judgment. In light of this truth, what should we do? Read the points below and scripture, and write down any questions you have to discuss in our next session.

1.   Fear God, not man (Luke 12:4–5).

2.   Turn from your sin and trust in Jesus, for He alone "delivers us from the wrath to come" (1 Thessalonians 1:10).

3.   Love God, not the things of the world (2 Peter 3:10–13).

4.   Do not count your life too dear (Acts 20:22–24).

5.   Do not be surprised by persecution, but rejoice (1 Peter 4:12–14).

6.   In days of trouble, cry out to God in prayer and worship (Psalm 50:14–15).

7.   Set your hope on God (1 Corinthians 1:8–10).

NOTES

JONAH

JONAH: RUN TO GOD

By: Shauna Van Dyke
www.speakthetruth.org

JONAH

The Lord commanded the prophet Jonah to preach against the wickedness of Nineveh, the capital of the Assyrian Kingdom. Assyria was a ruthless and idolatrous nation. However, Jonah was stubborn and instead chose to flee to Tarshish, stating, "I knew that you are a gracious and compassionate God, slow to anger and abounding in love, a God who relents from sending calamity" (4:2). Jonah wanted justice his way for Nineveh to receive God's judgment by being destroyed. In the book of Jonah, we learn how to respond to the will of God and how to share the love and mercy of God with others.

Have your counselee read the whole book of Jonah prior to your session and write out the things they learned about Jonah and about God. Note: There is a lot to cover within these four chapters, so you may not be able to cover all of it in one session. The questions below are just to get your conversation started as the Lord reveals more to you both.

IN SESSION COUNSELING

Discuss the takeaways that your counselee had about Jonah and about God. Take time to listen and discern their understanding. Ask questions such as the following:

- How would you summarize what happened in the book of Jonah?
- How would you describe Jonah?
- Did Jonah have reasons to be angry toward the Assyrians?
- What do you observe about Jonah's actions? How did God respond?
- In what ways do you relate to Jonah?
- What did you learn about God in this narrative?

Communicate your gratefulness in their sharing and then begin discussing the few points below to bring encouragement in their area of struggle.

What do we learn about Jonah?

Jonah was angry. Why? He didn't want to see God's mercy extended to his enemies. In his bitterness and pride he felt they were undeserving of His love, wanted justice his way and felt Nineveh should be destroyed. *Have you ever felt this about somebody?*

Jonah was disobedient. How? He was unfaithful to God's command and ran away in his pride and stubbornness. He felt spiritually superior and, in his grumbling, would have preferred to die than show them mercy. *Have you ever been disobedient to the Lord's command?*

Jonah was repentant. Where? In the belly of the whale. Despite his efforts to run away, the Lord was persistent and forgiving. Jonah expected to die but realized the Lord spared him. He prayed for God's help (2:1–2), he accepted God's discipline (2:3), he trusted God's promises (2:4–7), and yielded to God's will (2:8–9). Jonah couldn't save himself, but the goodness of God brings him to repentance. So, we see Jonah go from rebellion to repentance. *When have you gone from rebellion to repentance? Is there anything you need to repent of now?*

JONAH

What do we learn about God?

God is sovereign. God will accomplish what He wants through us, despite our objections or procrastination. How much easier it would be if we, unlike Jonah, would submit to Him without delay!

God is omnipresent. We cannot hide from God, He is always with us. Despite Jonah's attempt to run away, God was with him in his obedience and disobedience.

God is gracious. He disciplines Jonah through his disobedience. He hears him (4:1–4), comforts him (4:5–8), teaches him (4:9–11), and restores his ministry. Jonah, a man who lacked compassion for people who would perish and live eternally apart from God, was still used to bring a whole city to faith in the Lord.

God is merciful. Nineveh, an enemy of Israel, y had moved away from God and into idolatry. The people were wicked yet the Lord magnified his sovereignty and showed them love and mercy. No matter how awful our sin, we can be spared judgment like the Ninevites if we seek God's mercy and choose the path of humility and repentance.

AFTER SESSION ASSIGNMENT
Read Jonah again this week and reflect on the things we discussed in session. Journal through the questions below as the Lord continues to reveal areas for growth.

1. How are you encouraged knowing that God has a plan for you according to His purpose and will accomplish it? Read Ephesians 2:4–10 and Romans 8:28.

2. Read Proverbs 18:10. Do you tend to run away from the Lord? Run *to* the Lord, not away *from* Him.

3. Do you struggle with pride? Are you ever impatient with others who are spiritually ignorant or immature? Wanting justice in your own way, in your own timing?

4. How can you practically begin trusting the Lord and run to Him when you have been wronged, become angry, and desire worldly justice?

5. Is there someone in your life that God might be using to get your attention, like the men on the boat?

6. Read 2 Peter 3:9. Do you need to seek God's mercy and repent? Is there someone else in your life that you can show God's mercy and help them with their struggle in sin/disobedience?

NOTES

NOTES